Christmas in Minutes

Christmas in Minutes

Festive crafts in less than an hour

carol cox
josie cameron

GEORGETOWN
PUBLICATIONS

First published in 2003 in Canada by
Georgetown Publications Inc.

GEORGETOWN
PUBLICATIONS

579 Richmond Street West
Suite 100,
Toronto, Ontario
M5V 1Y6

ISBN 0-9731994-1-5

Printed in China

10 9 8 7 6 5 4 3 2 1

Contents

Introduction

Christmas in Minutes is packed with exciting, creative projects to bring holiday fun to your home. From chairbacks to garlands, wreaths to gift tags, there is something to suit all tastes and abilities. A practical techniques section contains step-by-step photographs for essential techniques—learn how to wire nuts, moss wreaths, and create triple ribbon bows with simple, easy-to-follow instructions.

Projects are arranged in sections according to the time required to complete them—15 minutes or less, 30 minutes or less, and 45 minutes or less. Make pretty decorated place cards for dinner guests in under 15 minutes, a striking calla lily centerpiece in less than 30 minutes, or a fragrant cinnamon door ring in under 45 minutes! However little time you have to spare, *Christmas in Minutes* will allow you to create beautiful decorations to make your home come alive with festive cheer.

Projects to make in

15 minutes or less

Ribbon rosettes

YOU WILL NEED

for each rosette

20" (50 cm) wire-edged ribbon,

  2" (5 cm) wide

know how to

1 Gently pull one of the wires at the edge of the piece of ribbon, and tie a knot in it.

2 At the other end of the ribbon but on the same edge, pull the wire and push the ribbon fabric along it, so that it gathers. Once the gathered edge of the ribbon reaches a length of approximately 8" (20 cm), tie a knot in the wire to hold the gathers in place.

3 Holding the end of the ribbon that has the first knot in it, roll the ribbon up, taking care to keep the gathered edges parallel.

4 Secure the roll by taking the knotted wire ends and wrapping them around the bottom of the roll, just above the gathered edge. Gently bend the top, ungathered edge of the ribbon roll to form a rosette.

know how long   5 minutes

Bay leaf and rosemary gift tags

YOU WILL NEED

Scissors

Cream-colored card

Bay leaves, 2 for each tag

Hole punch

Thin gift tag ribbon

Gold- or silver-ink pen

Rosemary sprigs, 2 for each tag

know how to

1 To make the bay leaf gift tags, cut a piece of card into the shape of one of the leaves. Stack the card between two bay leaves, and carefully punch a hole through the three layers at one end.

2 Thread some gift tag ribbon through the punched holes, and write a name on the card. Tie the gift tag to the gift.

3 To make the rosemary gift tags, cut a long oblong of card, roughly the same shape as the rosemary sprigs. Punch a hole through one end of it.

4 Thread some gift tag ribbon through the hole in the card, then gently push the sprigs of rosemary through the same hole. Their leaves should hold them in place. Write a name on the card, and tie the tag to the gift.

know how long 10 minutes

Raffia bow and knot

YOU WILL NEED

1 bundle raffia

24 cinnamon sticks

Scissors

know how to

1 To make the bow seen in the foreground, layer about 15 raffia strands and fold the ends over to make a bow shape, following the technique for ribbon bows on page 81, but using a single piece of raffia rather than a stem wire to secure the bow shape.

2 Gather a bundle of 12 cinnamon sticks, and wind a single piece of raffia around them three or four times. Carefully thread one end of the raffia through the binding of the raffia bow, then tie the ends together at the back of the stick bundle.

3 To make the raffia knot, simply wind some strands of raffia around a bundle of 12 cinnamon sticks, and tie in a neat double knot at the front. Trim off the ends of the raffia to neaten them.

know how long   10 minutes

Decorated place cards

YOU WILL NEED

for each card

Thick white card, approximately 6" × 3" (15 × 8 cm)

Ruler

Scissors

Decoration: a selection from hazelnuts, dried rosebuds, ribbon bows, dried hydrangea, gilded ivy leaves, Douglas pine, ruscus leaves

Glue

Gold-ink pen

know how to

1 Lay the card on a flat surface with the long side facing you. Using a ruler and scissors, make a vertical score in the card approximately 1" (2.5 cm) from the short right-hand edge.

2 Gently bend the right-hand edge of the card up toward you so that it folds neatly along the score line. Turn the card over, so that the fold is on your left, with the flap tucked underneath.

3 Decorate the bottom right-hand corner of the card by gluing in place a combination of pretty items.

4 Write your guest's name diagonally on the left-hand side of the card, and use the folded-under edge to prop the place card up on your guest's sideplate.

know how long 10 minutes

Candy pots

YOU WILL NEED

for each pot

1 small aluminum bucket

10 foil-wrapped candies

1 triple ribbon bow (see page 82 for technique)

Double-sided tape

know how to

1 Fill the bucket with a variety of different colored candies, arranging them so that there is a variety of color and the foil wrappings are displayed to advantage.

2 Attach a triple ribbon bow to the top of the bucket with double-sided tape

know how long   10 minutes

Sheaf and bow door decoration

YOU WILL NEED

3 small sprigs Douglas pine

2 small sprigs holly
   with berries

1 × 28-gauge (0.38 mm)
   stem wire

1 ready-made twig bow,
   sprayed gold

1 yard (91 cm) ribbon

know how to

1 Gather the pine sprigs into a neat bundle, then place the holly sprigs on top, gathering the stems into the bundle.

2 Wind a stem wire tightly around the bundle of pine and holly three times, about 1" (2.5 cm) from the ends of the stems.

3 Bring the wires to the front of the sheaf, and push them through the central "knot" of the twig bow. Twist the wires around the center of the bow to secure the sheaf to it.

4 Wind the ribbon around the center of the twig bow two or three times, leaving two equal lengths of ribbon. Knot the ribbon at the top of the bow, then again at the ends to create a long loop with which to hang the decoration.

know how long   15 minutes

Hazelnut hearth decoration

YOU WILL NEED

Glue gun

2 heads dried red hydrangea,
separated into 6 florets

1 quarter log with bark,
approximately 1 foot (30 cm)
long

4 small ivy trails, sprayed lightly
with fast-drying gold spray

15 hazelnuts, sprayed lightly
with fast-drying gold spray

know how to

1 Glue the six hydrangea florets onto the quarter log, bark-side up, two at each end and two toward the center of the log.

2 Place the trails of gilded ivy on the log, winding them among the hydrangea florets, and glue them in place.

3 Glue small clusters of hazelnuts to the log so that they nestle among the ivy and hydrangea, leaving some of the bark showing.

know how long 15 minutes

Bauble centerpiece

YOU WILL NEED

**Selection of silver and gold
    ornaments**

Footed glass bowl

**Set of white, shadeless
    Christmas lights**

know how to

1 Arrange a layer of ornaments in the bottom of the bowl.

2 Begin threading the lights between the ornaments, carefully weaving the cord around them. Add more ornaments and wind the lights around these, too. Take time to make sure the lights are evenly distributed.

3 Finish the arrangement with a layer of ornaments, hiding as much of the electrical cord as you can.

know how long   15minutes

Leaf-wrapped candle

YOU WILL NEED

2 magnolia leaves

Double-sided tape

1 pillar candle, approximately
   4" (10 cm) tall

Cream and gold cord, long
   enough to wrap around the
   candle three times

4 pins

know how to

1 Place the two magnolia leaves together, and cut off the stalks, so that the leaves are the same length and slightly shorter than the candle.

2 Stick a piece of double-sided tape to the underside of both leaves, and gently press them in place on the candle. The cut edges should line up with the candle's base, and the sides of the leaves should overlap an equal amount on both sides.

3 Fold the cream and gold cord in half. Tie a knot in the middle of the double cord. Wrap the cord around the candle, with the decorative knot in the center of one of the leaves. Trim off the excess cord and pin the ends neatly to the back of the candle.

know how long   15 minutes

Dried rose ornaments

YOU WILL NEED

for each ornament

Scissors

20 dried roses

7" (18 cm) gold-wrapped wire

Dry florist's foam ball, 1¼"
(3 cm) in diameter

Gold glitter spray

know how to

1 Cut the stems of the roses ¾" (2 cm) from the heads.

2 Thread the length of gold-wrapped wire through the dry florist's foam ball, bending ½" (1 cm) of it back into the ball at the base.

3 Push the roses into the florist's foam ball as close to each other as possible, until no florist's foam can be seen.

4 Spray the finished ornament with gold glitter spray for a touch of festive sparkle.

know how long   15 minutes

Projects to make in

30 minutes or less

Dried apple ring

YOU WILL NEED

70 dried red apple slices
  (see page 84 for technique)

1 yard (91 cm) spool wire

5 feet (1.5 m) ribbon

know how to

1 Make a sharp bend in the wire approximately 4" (10 cm) from one end. Thread the other end of the wire through the center of the apple slices, leaving about 4" (10 cm) of wire bare.

2 Twist the two wire ends together to hold the slices in place, and make a small loop from which to hang the ring.

3 Cut the ribbon into four equal lengths. Tie each piece of ribbon in a bow on the apple ring, one at the top, one at the bottom, and one at each side.

know how long   20 minutes

Ribbon garlands

YOU WILL NEED

for a 20" (50 cm) garland

**20 pieces of assorted ribbon,
8" (20 cm) long**

Fabric adhesive

know how to

1 Glue the ends of the first ribbon together with fabric adhesive, to form a ring.

2 Place the second ribbon through the first ring, then glue the ends together to make a second ring, interlinked with the first.

3 Repeat until all the pieces of ribbon have been used.

know how long   20 minutes

Berry heart chairback

YOU WILL NEED

Approximately 2 yards (182 cm)
    fine copper wire

Wire heart, 8" (20 cm) wide

25 to 30 small sprigs of berries

Strong scissors or wire cutters

5 ruscus leaves

20" (50 cm) red ribbon

know how to

1   Wind the end of the copper wire around the top of the heart frame. Place a sprig of berries on the heart, and wrap the wire around it diagonally once or twice.

2   Add a second sprig, and continue winding the wire around the heart to secure it. When the heart is covered, wind the wire around the frame to secure it and snip off the end.

3   Wire two berry sprigs together, leaving the wire ends long. Glue the ruscus leaves in a star shape around the berries, their stems overlapping. Poke both wire ends through the leaves, and twist them together at the back to hold the leaves in place.

4   Bring the ends of the wire up to the central dip in the heart and wind them around it to hold the central leaf and berry decoration in place. Thread a ribbon through the hanging loop and tie the chairback to a chair.

know how long   25 minutes

Festive pinecones

YOU WILL NEED

Pinecones (enough to fill the bowl)

Old newspaper

Fast-drying snow spray

Silver glitter

Display bowl

know how to

1 Lay the pinecones on the newspaper in a well-ventilated room.

2 Spray them with the snow spray. Sprinkle glitter over the cones immediately, before the spray has time to dry.

3 Gently turn each cone over and repeat step 2. Leave to dry.

4 Once the cones are dry enough to handle, arrange them in your bowl.

know how long   25 minutes

Dried cranberry bells

YOU WILL NEED

for each bell

2 × 28-gauge (0.38 mm) stem
wires

4 oz. (110 g) dried cranberries

1 large silver bead

6" (15 cm) silver string

12" (30 cm) fine wired tinsel

know how to

1 Lay the stem wires across each other to form a cross, and twist one around the other to hold the shape in place. About 1" (2.5 cm) from the central twist, bend each wire upward to form a gentle curve.

2 Thread cranberries onto each wire, leaving the last 2½" (7 cm) of wire bare.

3 Bring opposite wires toward each other and twist them together directly above the cranberries so that two intersecting triangles are formed. Gently adjust the wires to make a bell shape.

4 Thread the bead onto the silver string and tie it around the point where the wires intersect at the top of the bell, so that the bead dangles in the center. Wrap the end of the fine wired tinsel around the top intersection to secure it, then form a loop in the loose end from which to hang the decoration.

know how long 25 minutes

Amaryllis tree

YOU WILL NEED

7 white amaryllis

String

Scissors

Jar that fits into the outer pot,

  large enough to hold the stems

White ceramic pot

1 handful Spanish moss

2 long trails gilded ivy

know how to

1 Grasp an amaryllis stem near the flower head in one hand. Arrange the other stems around the first, taking care to position each flower so that it fits snugly next to the other blooms without overlapping them.

2 Tie a piece of string around the stems, just under the flower heads, to hold them in place. Arrange the stems so that they form a trunk, and tie another piece of string around the bottom. Cut the ends of the stems to the same length.

3 Place the amaryllis tree inside the jar. Then place the jar inside the white ceramic container and fill it almost to the brim with water. Use Spanish moss to fill the space between the stems and the ceramic container, hiding the inner jar.

4 Push the ends of the ivy trails between the amaryllis stems just under the flower heads, then wind them around the stems.

know how long   30 minutes

Lichen and lime ring

YOU WILL NEED

1 florist's foam ring, 8" (20 cm) in
   diameter

6 to 8 large handfuls natural
   lichen

12 to 15 florist's wire pins

4 lime green gauze ribbon bows
   (see page 81 for technique)

4 fresh lime peel roses (see page
   90 for technique)

Cream-colored pillar candle,
   5" (13 cm) high, to fit in center
   of ring

know how to

1 Place the foam ring on a flat surface. Take a handful of lichen
and secure it to the ring with florist's wire pins. Continue in
this way until the ring is covered.

2 Place the bows evenly around the ring, securing them by
pushing their wire "tails" into the foam through the moss.

3 Take the lime peel roses and push their securing wires into the
foam, in between the bows.

4 Place the candle in the middle of the ring.

know how long   30 minutes

Calla lily centerpiece

YOU WILL NEED

Wide glass bowl

18 to 20 long, slim green leaves

Knife

½ block wet florist's foam

18 deep red calla lilies

Scissors

Christmas lights

know how to

1 Lay 12 leaves in the bowl so that their tips overlap the rim very slightly. Cut the wet florist's foam with a knife so that it fits snugly in the bottom of the bowl. Push it firmly into the bowl on top of the leaves to hold them in place.

2 Cut the stem of the first calla lily so that the tip of the flower just overlaps the rim of the bowl when it is laid on top of one of the leaves. Continue in this way, using 12 of the lilies evenly spaced around the edge of the bowl.

3 Poke the stems of the remaining lilies into the oasis so that they fan out in the center of the arrangement. Fill any gaps with the remaining leaves, cutting them so that they are slightly shorter than the lilies.

4 Place the arrangement on the table, and wind Christmas lights around the base of the bowl. This uplighting effect will show the beautiful color combination of the flowers and leaves to its best advantage.

know how long   30 minutes

Pink rose tree

YOU WILL NEED

Scissors

12 pink roses, foliage and thorns
   removed

½ block wet florist's foam

1 silver-colored pot
   approximately 5" (12 cm) tall

String

2 handfuls green reindeer moss

Florist's wire pins

2 feet (60 cm) festive ribbon

know how to

1 Cut the rose stems to 10" (25 cm) and place in deep water, almost up to the base of the flower heads, for at least 10 minutes before using. Meanwhile cut the wet florist's foam to fit snugly in the silver-colored pot.

2 Gather the bunch of roses in one hand, and with the other hand arrange them so the flowers form a half sphere and the stems sit snugly together. Tie a piece of string around the stems, just under the flower heads, to hold them firmly in place.

3 If necessary, trim the ends of the stems so that they are flush with each other, then push the bundle firmly into the florist's foam in the pot. Push moss into the pot to hide the florist's foam, securing it with florist's wire pins.

4 Wrap the ribbon around the stems to hide the string and add some festive glitz.

know how long 30 minutes

Lavender and petal candle holders

YOU WILL NEED

Dried lavender flowers

Aluminum foil

Glass candle holders

Glue

Dried hydrangea petals

know how to

1 To make the lavender candle holder, spread lavender flowers evenly over a sheet of aluminum foil.

2 Cover the outside of the glass container with a thin layer of glue, then roll the glass in the lavender until it is completely coated. Leave to dry.

3 To make the hydrangea candle holder, apply a thin line of glue around the top of the candle and carefully place a row of petals on it, overlapping each petal with the next.

4 Below this row, add another thin line of glue and add the next row of petals, overlapping the top row as well as the individual petals. Repeat for each row of petals until you reach the bottom of the glass. Leave to dry.

know how long 30minutes

Projects to make in

Pinecone and pomegranate wreath

YOU WILL NEED

12 to 15 sprigs pine

Florist's wire pins

Mossed wreath (see page 88 for technique)

24 cinnamon sticks

35 stem wires

Raffia

5 dried orange slices (see page 84 for technique)

5 pomegranates, lightly sprayed gold

2 small red apples

18 pinecones, lightly sprayed gold

10 to 12 rosemary sprigs

5 dried red flowers

5 pieces shaved pine

Bow (see page 81 for the technique)

know how to

1 Lay the pine sprigs on the wreath so that they overlap, and secure them with florist's wire pins.

2 Make six bundles of cinnamon sticks by wrapping a stem wire around each, and twisting the ends together. Tie strands of raffia over the wire on each bundle. Push the wire tails through the wreath and bend them to hold the bundles in place.

3 Attach the dried fruit and the pinecones following the method described in step 2.

4 Poke rosemary sprigs into the wreath and place the dried flowers and pine shavings among the pine sprigs. Pass a stem wire through the bow and attach it securely to the wreath.

know how long 35 minutes

Calla lily flower tree

YOU WILL NEED

Slim cylindrical vase

Small piece wet florist's foam

10 to 12 deep red calla lilies

4 to 5 leaves approximately

2" (5 cm) wide and longer than

6" (15 cm)

18" (45 cm) festive ribbon

know how to

1 Choose a vase into which 10 to 12 calla lily stems will fit snugly. Place wet florist's foam in the bottom so that it occupies about one-third of the container. This will help hold the lily stems steady. Add enough water to fill half of the vase.

2 Trim the stems of the lilies so that the flower heads begin approximately 7" (18 cm) above the base of the vase, taking into account the florist's foam at the bottom of it.

3 Place the lilies in the vase, with the pointed ends of the flowers facing outward. Cut the leaves to 6" (15 cm) and secure them around the container, pointed ends up, with festive ribbon.

know how long **35**minutes

Clove-studded and carved limes

YOU WILL NEED

8 to 10 perfect limes

Pencil

Whole dried cloves

Linoleum cutter

Footed glass bowl

know how to

1 To make the clove-studded limes, take a pencil and lightly mark the pattern you want to follow on the limes. Using the lines as a guide, press cloves into the limes, keeping the cloves as close together as possible.

2 To make the carved limes, use the pencil to draw simple patterns. With the linoleum cutter, and using the lines as a guide, gently score out the lime peel, revealing the pith but making sure you cut no deeper.

3 Arrange the studded and carved limes in a footed glass bowl for a deliciously aromatic centerpiece.

know how long   35 minutes

Silver twig tree

YOU WILL NEED
Block of florist's foam
Square dull-silver container,
   approximately 5" (13 cm) wide
   and 6" (15 cm) high
Scissors
15 well-branched twigs, sprayed
   evenly with fast-drying silver
   spray
Blue bead decorations on loops
Small blue ribbon bows (see
   page 81 for technique)

know how to

1 Cut the florist's foam so that it fits inside the container.

2 Cut the silver twigs so that they are approximately 18" (45 cm) in length, and poke each one firmly into the florist's foam, beginning in the center with the largest twig.

3 Place the bead decorations on the branches so that they are distributed evenly.

4 Make four small bows and push the long wire of each bow into each corner of the tin.

know how long 35 minutes

Nut and holly centerpiece

YOU WILL NEED

Florist's tape

½ block wet florist's foam

Shallow tray large enough to
hold the florist's foam

Silver dish

3 taper candles, approximately
8" (20 cm) tall

Small bunch round-leaf holly

6 to 8 sprigs Douglas pine

Assorted wired nuts (see page
83 for technique), sprayed
with gold and copper
fast-drying metallic paint

Green reindeer moss

know how to

1 Tape the florist's foam into the tray, then place the tray on the silver plate. Poke the candles firmly into the center of the florist's foam.

2 Add the sprigs of holly and pine, poking them firmly into the florist's foam around the top and sides, so that some sprigs rest on the table.

3 Push the wired nuts into the florist's foam so that they nestle among the foliage. Push in small clumps of reindeer moss to hide any florist's foam that is still showing.

know how long   35 minutes

Orange rose chairback

YOU WILL NEED

Florist's tape

Wet florist's foam, soaked, to fit
   in holder

Florist's foam holder 6" × 4"
   (15 × 10 cm) with short handle

Scissors

12 orange roses

12 to 15 ivy trails in assorted
   lengths from 4" to 10"
   (10 to 25 cm)

12 to 15 sprigs fresh rosemary in
   assorted lengths from 4" to 10"
   (10 to 25 cm)

18" (45 cm) spool wire

2 feet (60 cm) orange ribbon

know how to

1 Tape the soaked florist's foam to the holder, so that it cannot
fall out of the holder once hung on the back of a chair.

2 Cut the orange roses to approximately 6" (12 cm) and strip off
any thorns or foliage. Push the first rose stem into the center of
the florist's foam so that the stem is at right angles to it. Push
the rest of the roses in at slight angles so that they fan out
toward the edges.

3 Fill in the spaces between the roses with ivy and rosemary,
working from the center outward, using the longer pieces
toward the edges.

4 Thread the spool wire through the handle of the florist's foam
holder and use it to attach the chairback to the chair. Tie a bow
around the spool wire to hide it.

know how long   40 minutes

Pine and chilli wall hanging

YOU WILL NEED

Scissors

1 yard (91 cm) pale green voile

Florist's wire pins

Moss-filled chicken wire frame
(see page 92 for technique),
approximately 12" × 4"
(30 × 10 cm)

4 branches viburnum or other
foliage with small flowers, cut
into 2" (5 cm) pieces

20 chillies on long stalks

2 large branches Douglas pine,
cut into 2" (5 cm) pieces

15 to 20 28-gauge (0.38 mm)
stem wires

know how to

1 Cut the voile fabric in half lengthwise to make two long strips. Pin the first strip around the edge of the frame, so that it gathers together, creating a soft edge. Tuck the ends into the back of the frame.

2 Group and wire together small bunches of viburnum, chillies and pine (see page 91 for technique). Push them through the frame, securing them to the chicken wire at the back. Continue until the frame is covered.

3 With a stem wire and the remaining piece of voile, make a bow (see page 81 for technique) and attach it to the bottom of the frame. Use a second stem wire to make a loop at the top of the frame from which to hang the wall hanging.

know how long 40 minutes

Decorated tealight holders

YOU WILL NEED

for 3 holders

3 stems rosemary,
   approximately 12" (30 cm) long

3 glass tealight holders

12 to 15 30-gauge (0.32 mm)
   stem wires

18 small sprigs small red
   berries, 2 to 4 berries per sprig

Scissors

3 tealight candles

know how to

1 Wind a rosemary stem tightly around the top of one of the tealight holders, overlapping the ends. Join the ends together by wrapping a stem wire around them four or five times. Remove from the glass.

2 Attach six berry sprigs around the rosemary ring with stem wires, spacing them evenly and snipping off any extra wire.

3 Place a tealight inside the holder and replace the rosemary and berry ring around the top. Repeat steps 1 to 3 for the other two holders.

know how long   40 minutes

Cinnamon door ring

YOU WILL NEED

16 ivy strands, half of them gilded, 3 to 5 feet (1 to 1.5 m) long

1 mossed wreath (see page 88 for technique)

10 to 12 florist's wire pins

20 to 25 28-gauge (0.38 mm) stem wires

18 to 20 cinnamon sticks

2 dried orange bundles (see page 84 for technique)

9 golden spherical ornaments

3 to 4 handfuls Spanish moss

4 festive bows, 2 small and 2 medium (see page 81 for technique)

Coordinating ribbon rosette made from double-sided ribbon (see page 10 for technique)

2 feet (60 cm) ribbon for hanging door ring

know how to

1 Wind strands of green and gold ivy around the mossed wreath, securing them with florist's wire pins.

2 Make two bundles of cinnamon sticks by wrapping a stem wire around each, and twisting the ends together. Wrap a piece of ribbon over the wire and tie it firmly next to the twisted wire tails. Push the wire tails through to the back of the wreath and bend to hold the cinnamon bundles in place. Attach dried orange bundles and gold ornaments in the same way.

3 Attach the bows to the top of the ring, the small ones on top of the medium-sized ones, and wire the rosette into the center of them. Thread the ribbon through the top of the ring.

know how long 45minutes

Eucalyptus garland

YOU WILL NEED

Spool wire

Mossed rope, 2 yards
   (182 cm) long
   (see page 86 for technique)

6 small branches Douglas pine,
   approximately 2 feet
   (60 cm) long

8 stems eucalyptus

Scissors

7 ribbon bows (see page 81
   for technique)

7 dried apple bundles (see
   page 84 for technique)

7 gold-sprayed terracotta pots,
   1½" (4 cm) tall

7 × 28-gauge (0.38 mm) stem wires

7 clumps green reindeer moss

know how to

1 Tie the end of the spool wire around one end of the mossed rope. Take a branch of pine and lay it along the rope.

2 Wind the spool wire around the pine diagonally and, as you approach the tip of the branch, tuck a eucalyptus stem behind it and continue winding. Alternate pine and eucalyptus in this way until the rope is covered.

3 Add clusters of bows and dried apple bundles to the garland by poking their wires through to the back of the rope and twisting them together.

4 Attach the terracotta pots by inserting a stem wire through the hole at the bottom and pushing both ends through the rope, twisting at the back to secure. Fill each pot with moss.

know how long   45 minutes

Practical techniques

In the following pages you will find simple instructions for the essential techniques used in the *Christmas in Minutes* projects. Each technique is clearly illustrated with step–by–step photographs, and includes a useful cross-reference to the project or projects for which it is needed. In the case of some techniques, such as drying fruit, you may wish to make a large batch for use over several months and several projects.

In the photograph below are some of the basic materials and equipment used in the projects. Items are available from hardware stores, craft stores, and florist's stores.

Center: *dried orange and apple slices*

Clockwise from top left: *chicken wire, gold-sprayed walnuts, moss, strong scissors, thick nylon string, spool wire, mini terracotta pots sprayed gold, 20-gauge (0.90 mm) stem wires, wire wreath ring, 28-gauge (0.38 mm) stem wires, florist's tape, glue gun, low-melt glue sticks, cream-and-gold colored cord, red-and-gold colored wire-edged ribbon, green wire-edged ribbon, blue wire-edged ribbon.*

useful know how # Simple ribbon bows

YOU WILL NEED

12" (30 cm) ribbon

1 × 28-gauge (0.38 mm) stem wire

1 Lay the ribbon on a flat surface and cross over the two ends so that they overlap in the center.

2 Pinch the central point where the ribbon ends cross.

3 Place the stem wire at the back of the pinched point and wrap it tightly around the bow. Leave the ends of the stem wire to attach it to the relevant project.

Used in:

Raffia bow and knot, p.14; Lichen and lime ring, p.48; Silver twig tree, p.64; Pine and chilli wall hanging, p.72; Cinnamon door ring, p.76; Eucalyptus garland, p.78.

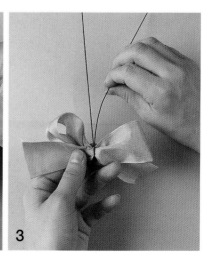

useful know how # Triple ribbon bows

YOU WILL NEED

1 yard (91 cm) wire-edged ribbon

1 × 28-gauge (0.38 mm) stem wire

1 Arrange the ribbon in a zigzag shape so that there are three loops on each side, each loop shorter than the last.

2 Push the layers together and pinch them in the center. Wrap a 28-gauge (0.38 mm) stem wire tightly around the bow, and twist the ends together at the back, behind the longest layer, to hold it in place.

3 Wrap the end of the ribbon at the front of the bow over the wire, around the center of the bow. Repeat this with the ribbon end from the back of the bow. The wired edges of the ribbon should hold the ends in place.

Used in: Candy pots, p.18.

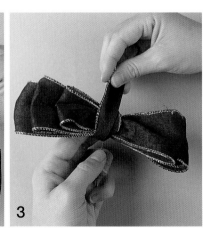

useful know how # Wired nuts

YOU WILL NEED

Assorted nuts

28-gauge (0.38 mm) stem wires,
   one for each nut

Hot glue gun

1 Make a small loop at the top of a stem wire.

2 Dab a small amount of hot glue onto a nut and press it onto the circle of wire. Leave to harden.

3 To wire walnuts, simply push a stem wire into the nut at the bottom of the shell where there is a tiny hole. Dab a small amount of hot glue around the hole to hold the wire in place.

Used in: Nut and holly centerpiece, p.66.

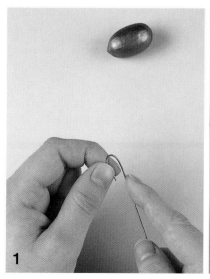
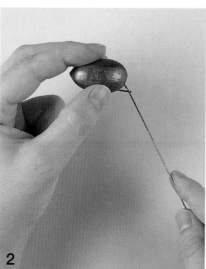

useful know how # Dried fruit bundles

YOU WILL NEED

Sharp knife

Crisp apples

Oranges

Baking tray

Aluminum foil

1 × 28-gauge (0.38 mm) stem
wire for each bundle

1 Cut each fruit into thin slices, approximately ¼" (5 mm) in width, using a sharp knife.

2 Lay the slices on a baking tray covered with aluminum foil, making sure that none of the slices are touching. Bake for six to eight hours at the lowest setting on your oven. Check the slices every hour or so to make sure that they do not burn.

3 Once the slices have cooled, group three or four together and push a stem wire through them about one-third of the way up from the bottom.

4 Bend the ends of the wire downward and twist them together to hold the slices in place. They should naturally separate from each other, forming an attractive ornament.

Used in:
Dried apple ring, p.34; Cinnamon door ring, p.76;
Eucalyptus garland, p.78.

useful know how # Mossed rope

YOU WILL NEED

Thick nylon string, the required
length of the finished rope plus
10" (25 cm)

Spool wire

5 handfuls moss per 1 foot
(30 cm) nylon string

1 Make a loop about 2" (5 cm) long at the both ends of the nylon string.

2 Tie the end of the spool wire to the string, at the bottom of one of the loops.

3 Press a small clump of moss on and around the string. Wind the spool wire over the moss and down the string to hold the moss in place. Continue adding clumps of moss and winding the spool wire around it to the end of the string.

4 Cut the spool wire leaving an end of 3" (8 cm). Wind this end tightly around the final loop in the string, and tuck it in.

Used in:
Eucalyptus garland, p.78.

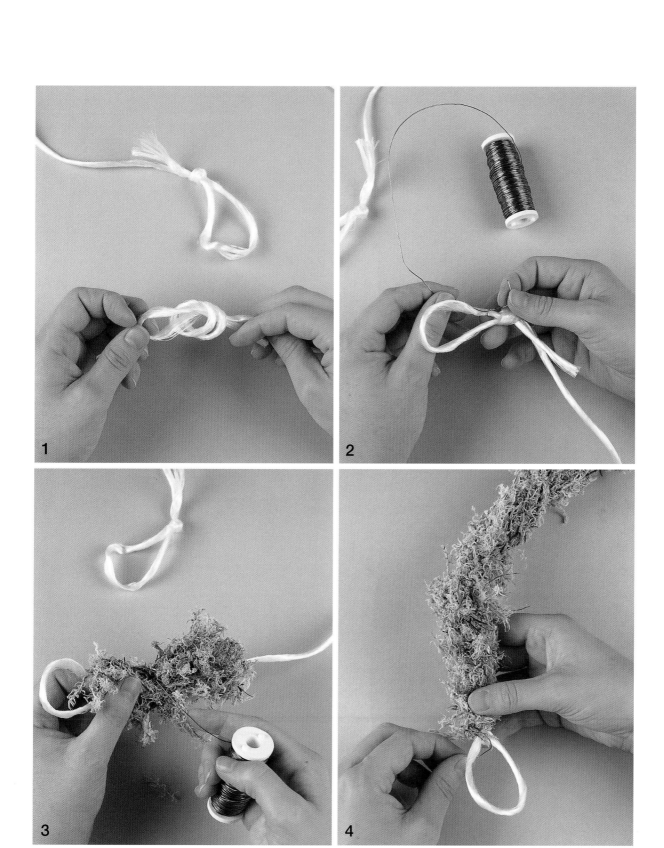

useful know how # Mossed wreath

YOU WILL NEED

1 wire wreath ring, 12" (30 cm)
  in diameter

12 to 14 large handfuls moss

Spool wire

1 Wind the end of the spool wire onto the edge of the wire ring to hold it in place.

2 Bind a handful of moss to the ring by holding it in place and winding the spool wire around it. Add more moss and wind wire round it and the ring until the whole ring is covered.

3 Cut the spool wire, leaving an end of 3" (8 cm), and wind the end around the edge of the wire ring to hold it in place.

4 Trim off any long, straggly pieces of moss to neaten the ring.

Used in:

Cinnamon door ring, p.76.

useful know how # Lime peel roses

YOU WILL NEED   **1 × 28-gauge (0.38 mm) stem**
Unblemished green limes, 1 for   **wire for each rose**
each rose
Sharp knife or vegetable peeler

1 Starting at one end of the lime, carefully peel it with a
vegetable peeler or sharp knife, so that the outer skin comes
off in one complete coiled piece.

2 Very gently wind one end of the peel back on itself, in the
opposite direction of its natural curve, so that the pith is on the
outside. Continue winding until you reach the other end.

3 Push a stem wire through the end and through the layers of
peel so that is comes out in the center. Bend the wires
downward and twist them together.

Used in:
Lichen and lime ring, p.48.

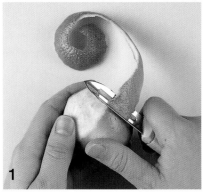

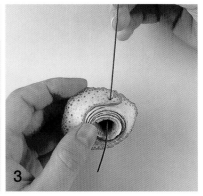

useful know how # Bunches of berries, chillies, or pine

YOU WILL NEED

Berries, chillies, or pine cut into small pieces or clusters approximately 2" (5 cm) long

Scissors

1 × 20-gauge (0.90 mm) stem wire per bunch

1 Bend a stem wire in the center so that it resembles a large hairpin. Place it behind a group of three chillies, and hold the chillies and the bend of the wire in one hand.

2 With the other hand, firmly wrap one of the wire ends around the chilli stems and the other part of the wire. Leave the ends long to attach the bunch to the project. Make bunches of berries or pine in the same way.

Used in:

Pine and chilli wall hanging, p.72.

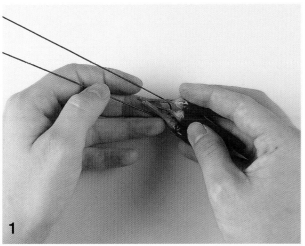

useful know how # Chicken wire frame

YOU WILL NEED

1 piece chicken wire, 12" × 14"
   (30 × 35 cm)

Three large handfuls moss

18" (45 cm) spool wire

1 Lay chicken wire on a flat surface and fold the longest edges together until they meet in the middle.

2 Stuff the moss inside the folded chicken wire.

3 Fold the ends over and press them down firmly.

4 Use the spool wire to "stitch" the edges of the chicken wire together. Tuck the ends into the moss.

Used in:

Pine and chilli wall hanging, p.72.

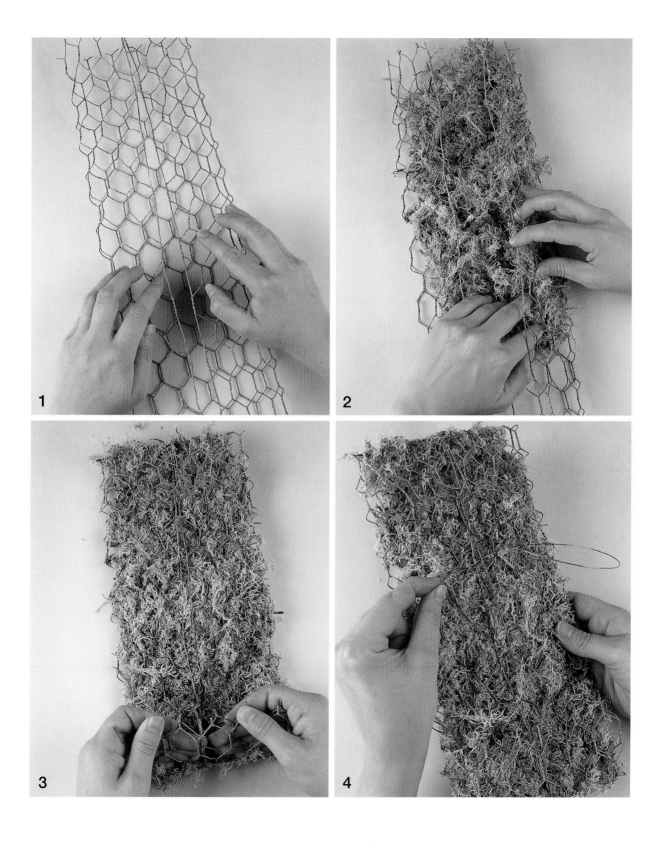

List of projects